MINERAL COMPOSITION OF GLUTEN, STARCH, AND WATER-SOLUBLES
FRACTIONS OF WHEAT FLOUR AND ITS RELATIONSHIP TO FLOUR QUALITY

by

ROBERT KESLER DEQUITTE

B. S., Montana State College, 1956

A THESIS

submitted in partial fulfillment of the

requirements of the degree

MASTER OF SCIENCE

Department of Flour and Food Milling Industries

KANSAS STATE COLLEGE
OF AGRICULTURE AND APPLIED SCIENCE

1958

TABLE OF CONTENTS

INTRODUCTION AND REVIEW OF LITERATURE

Mineral composition of wheat and flour is known to vary with environment and heredity. Environmental factors include weather, available nutrients in the soil and the physical condition of the soil. Beeson (5) and Bailey (3) have reviewed the extensive early literature on the mineral composition of wheat and flour. Many of these early analyses were carried out on samples of unknown origin and frequently information on soil, climatic factors, variety, and baking quality were lacking. Most results indicated the total ash and composition of the ash varied greatly.

Uptake of available nutrients by the wheat plant is affected by variety and soil moisture as well as the relative ratios of the elements in the soil (5). Greaves and Carter (17) found that the total ash in the grain increased progressively as the amount of irrigation water increased. Most of the increase resulted from additional phosphorus, potassium, calcium, and magnesium absorbed by the plants. In a later paper, Greaves, et. al. (16) reported that spring wheat contained greater percentages of total ash, calcium, potassium, iron, phosphorus, and sulfur than winter wheat grown on the same soil. This was assumed to be due to genetic differences between the two classes of wheats. Additions of green manure caused a significant increase in total ash, calcium, and phosphorus presumably because of the increased availability of these elements. No data on baking quality were reported.

Schrenk and King (36) reported that ash and mineral content of three wheat varieties grown for three years at 13 locations within the state of Kansas varied appreciably and were correlated, in general, with available nutrients in the soil. The availability of nutrients depended on the rain-

fall since high annual rainfall leached available nutrients from the soil.
Areas producing wheat with high mineral content also produced wheat with high
protein. Mineral content was influenced greatly by location, but only
slightly by variety. Areas producing high mineral content did so consistently,
indicating that differences due to rainfall and other environmental factors
during the three-year period did not affect mineral content significantly.
The increased ash content of Western Kansas wheats was not due to increases
in any one element, but was the result of combined increases in each of the
major constituents of the ash. The changes in minor element composition
showed no definite trend with respect to location.

In a continuation of this work, Schrenk (35) studied the effects of
calcium, magnesium, and phosphorus applications on the composition of grain
produced in Southeastern Kansas. The percentage of protein decreased due
to fertilizer treatment, while the mineral content of the grain increased.
This suggests that when non-nitrogenous fertilizers were applied at these
locations nitrogen content of the soil became a limiting factor. The most
noticeable effect of soil treatment was the increase in phosphorus content
of the grain. Magnesium decreased when only calcium and phosphorus were
applied to the soil. When these two nutrients were supplemented with
magnesium, magnesium also increased in the grain.

Information accumulated at the Hard Winter Wheat Quality Laboratory
(Finney, et. al., 12) and representing many varieties grown throughout the
Great Plains, indicates that total ash is controlled by two factors. These
are variety and environment, the most important of which is environment.
Variety plays a minor role in determining mineral content of whole wheat
under field conditions. Conditions that favor accumulation of protein in

the kernel generally favor accumulation of minerals.

Significant differences in the mineral composition of portions of the whole wheat kernel also have been measured. Morris, et. al. (27), employing a microdissection technique to separate whole wheat kernels into fractions, found evidence of an increasing gradient in ash and protein content extending outward from the center of the endosperm. Comparison of the ash and protein contents of the dissected fractions with those of Buhler flour mill streams of Thorne soft wheat showed that the dissected fraction with the lowest ash was identical with the flour stream with the lowest ash. The flour streams with the highest ash were slightly lower in ash than the dissected fractions with the highest ash. It is known generally that cations influence dough behavior and exert a modifying effect on the flour proteins (13, 25). Several methods of determining flour quality based on the measurement of physico-chemical properties of dispersed flour proteins have been shown to be affected by electrolytes present in wheat ash (Miller and Johnson, 25). Increasing the salt concentration of doughs prepared for testing in the Brabender Extensograph increases both the extensibility and resistance to extension of doughs. Weak and strong flours respond differently to added salt (Fisher, et. al., 13).

Water containing a medium degree of hardness is considered most suitable for baking purposes as some of the mineral salts have a strengthening effect on the gluten. Soft waters are objectionable in baking because they tend to yield a soft, sticky dough (Pylar, 33). Patented preparations generally are used to bring commercial doughs to a maximum ionic strength, regulated by the solubility of calcium sulfate.

Sullivan and Near (39) analyzed the ash of 20 wheat samples of widely

different character and origin and reported that magnesium content was
related directly to the strength of wheats as determined by protein
percentage and gluten quality. The gluten quality score was based on
physical properties of dough and washed gluten. This subjective method
of evaluating gluten quality leaves much to be desired.

Davidson and Shollenberger (6) studied effects on flour baking quality
of sodium nitrate applied at different stages during growth of the wheat
plant. Flour protein, ash, and absorption, loaf volume, and total loaf score
increased with increases in length of time from seeding until sodium
nitrate was applied. The highest flour protein, ash, and absorption, and
highest quality loaves resulted from application of sodium nitrate at
heading time.

Gericke (14, 15) grew wheat in hydroponic solutions and studied the
effects on bread scores of nitrate and chloride salts supplied during the
later period of plant growth. The quality of flour from wheat grown in
cultures where nitrogen was supplied in the form of ammonia was decidedly
inferior to that milled from wheat grown in cultures supplied with nitrogen
in the nitrate form. In both series, the use of calcium nitrate or chloride
resulted in higher bread scores than did the similar salts of potassium,
sodium, and magnesium. The use of ammonium nitrate resulted in the poorest
loaf produced from wheat grown in solutions containing different nitrate salts.
Some question of the validity of these results might be raised due to the
inadequacy of the baking tests used by Gericke. Although each sample was
baked by both basic and stimulated (diastased) methods, in several cases,
quality rankings varied between baking methods. Recently developed breadmaking methods (Finney, 9) are much better able to measure the breadmaking
potential of flours.

McCalla and Woodford (23) employed the liquid culture techniques of Gericke and reported that limiting the supply of potassium to wheat plants had an adverse effect on the quality of grain as determined by gluten and baking tests.

Separation of flour doughs or flour-water suspensions into their component complexes and reconstitution of these complexes to produce "synthetic" doughs has yielded considerable information on factors determining flour quality. Unfortunately, methods of making these separations have varied and some of the data obtained have been contradictory. The gluten complex, however, has been shown to be the most important substance in the flour. It is responsible for the elastic and cohesive properties of a flour dough and forms the three-dimensional network which is responsible for the characteristic porous structure of leavened bread. Pence, et. al. (30) and Sullivan (38) recently reviewed the literature on the role of wheat flour protein in baking.

Early workers separated gluten into fractions based on solubility in various solvents in an attempt to determine factors responsible for the unusual properties of gluten and the reasons for variation in properties of gluten obtained from different flours. The most important conclusion drawn from this work was that gluten consists of many components varying progressively in solubility and other physical properties (Miller and Johnson, 25).

Swanson (40) discussed the influence of electrolytes on the physical properties of doughs and on flour proteins. Doughs are influenced directly by the kind and amount of salt present, and indirectly by their effect on pH. Increase in viscosity of a dough in the presence of a salt was attributed to the appropriation of water by the salt molecules or ions. Decrease in viscosity would be caused by a dispersing effect on the gluten.

Few analyses of gluten obtained from flours of widely different dough characteristics and baking quality have shown significant differences in the amounts or kinds of amino acids. Miller, et. al. (26) studied the "microbiologically apparent" lysine, glutamic acid, cystine, and methionine content of whole wheats and found a relationship between mixing time and percent of both cystine and methionine as influenced by environment. No differences due to variety were observed. Flour from wheat samples high in cystine required the longest mixing for optimum dough development. Wöstmann (42) reported a positive correlation between flour strength, as reflected by surface area of extensograms, the cystine content of flour proteins, and total cystine content of the flour. Cystine was determined polarographically.

Present evidence indicates that variations in gluten properties, in part, are due to modifying influences exerted by the other dough complexes, mainly those materials extractable in water. Pence, et. al. (28, 29, 31) made detailed studies of effects of water-soluble flour components on baking behavior. They found that soluble pentosans had little effect on the baking performance of doughs reconstituted without the use of the water-soluble fraction of the flour, but the handling properties of the doughs were modified distinctly. These pentosans corrected to a large degree the softness, wet surface, and lack of normal stickiness shown in doughs reconstituted with only gluten and starch. Improvements in volume, grain, and texture, however, were small.

The soluble components of the flours were required for maximum performance of all glutens except that from a durum wheat, and appeared to be capable of affecting flour behavior to such an extent that differences or similarities in gluten characteristics were obscured. The pentosans of the crude albumin fraction (non-dialyzable portion of the water-solubles) were responsible for

the shortened mixing time of doughs containing this fraction. The amounts
of soluble proteins were found to increase directly with total flour
protein, but the relationship became inverse when they were expressed as
percentages of total protein. The ratio of albumins to globulins contained
by flours were correlated with protein quality beyond the one percent level
of significance. The authors postulated that albumin components act in a
beneficial manner in bread doughs, whereas, globulins act in a deleterious
manner. The resultant effect of the two proteins is reflected by the ratio
of their amounts.

Mattern and Sandstedt (22) reported that the principal factor responsible
for determining the mixing requirement of wheat flour is water-soluble. The
mixing time of a flour was lengthened by removal of the water-soluble fraction.
Reincorporation of the solubles reversed this effect. The mixing requirement of a flour also was extended by incorporating water extracted flour
with a normal flour.

Starch has been shown to exert some effect on dough properties and loaf
quality although these effects are rather small compared to those reported
for the gluten and water-soluble fractions. According to Sandstedt, et. al.
(34) the "amylodextrin" or "tailings starch" fraction of flour is a factor
in absorption and exerts its influence on the handling characteristics of
flour doughs. This material was associated with stickiness of doughs and
with tenderness of crumb in the baked product. Harris and Sibbit (18, 19)
found marked differences in the comparative baking qualities of starch
prepared from different wheat varieties. Synthetic flours were produced by
adding these starches to a constant gluten substrate at three protein levels.

Present evidence provided by Mattern and Sandstedt (22) leads to doubt

of the validity of early reports concerning the positive effects of starch
in determining dough characteristics and bread quality. Sandstedt, et. al.
(34) and Harris and Sibbit (19) separated the gluten and starch from a
dough mixed to optimum development and discarded the water-solubles.

In more recent work, (8, 22, 37, 43) the flour complexes have been
separated by methods designed to keep dough development at a minimum. Under
these conditions, the water-solubles are necessary in reconstituting a
"synthetic dough" which will result in bread of quality equal to that from a
normal flour.

Little is known about the relative distribution of the minerals in the
complexes separated from hydrated flours and their relationship to the
technological behavior of flour. El Cindy, et. al. (7) studied the influence
of variety, fertilizer treatment, and soil on the protein content and mineral
composition of wheat, flour, and flour fractions (gluten, starch, and water-
solubles). Milling behavior and flour yield were not affected noticeably
by soil differences or fertilizer treatments. Total wheat ash was affected
by fertilizer treatments and varied among varieties. The percentage of
specific elements in the ashes of the wheat and the flour fractions varied
greatly among varieties for some elements. There was no consistent
relationship among varieties and elemental composition compared as absolute
amounts or as percentages of the ash. The authors concluded that a complex
hereditary background probably influenced composition of the ash. No
information on the baking characteristics of these flours was presented.

The literature suggests that flour and gluten quality are controlled by
a factor or factors which are subtile in nature. One of these factors about
which there is little information is the mineral composition of flour and its

component parts and the relationship between mineral composition and baking
characteristics of the flours. The object of this study was to separate
hydrated flour into gluten, starch, and water-soluble complexes and to
correlated the results of mineral analyses of these fractions with baking
quality data.

MATERIALS AND METHODS

The flours used in this study consisted of 40 samples representing
five pure varieties of hard red winter wheat grown at eight locations in
Kansas in 1956. All wheat samples were milled to a straight-grade flour on
an Allis mill (Johnson, et. al., 20). Data pertaining to these samples are
presented in Table 1.

Moisture, ash, and protein were determined according to the methods of
the A. A. C. C. (1). Baking absorption was based on farinograph data
obtained using the constant flour weight method.

The straight-dough baking procedure was patterned after that described
by Finney (9). It was the same as that used by Miller, et. al. (24).

Mixograms were made according to the procedure of Johnson, et. al. (21).
They were measured using the method described by Swanson and Johnson (41).

The flour complexes or fractions were prepared by a modification of the
method developed by Finney (8). Details of this procedure are given in the
Appendix. The samples were ashed according to the procedure given in the
Appendix.

The mineral analyses were performed using both chemical and flame
photometric technics. Total phosphorus was determined by the reduced
molybdate colorimetric procedure of Pons, et. al. (32) (See Appendix). Iron

was determined according to the A.O.A.C. method (2) using alpha, alpha-dipyridyl as the complexing agent. Sodium, calcium, potassium, manganese, and magnesium were determined with a Beckman D. U. spectrophotometer equipped with flame photometry attachment and atomizer burner assembly (4). Details of the flame analysis procedure are given in the Appendix.

RESULTS AND DISCUSSION

Baking Quality

The protein and loaf volume data presented in Table 1 indicate that many of these flour samples contain protein of abnormal baking quality. An outstanding example of this is the comparison between protein content and loaf volumes of the samples grown at Hays and Belleville. The Hays samples averaged 16 percent protein and produced bread with an average loaf volume of 930 c.c. The Belleville samples averaged 12.8 percent protein and produced loaves averaging 943 c.c. The protein and loaf volume data of samples grown at Manhattan, Garden City, and Canton indicated that these samples also contained protein of inferior baking quality, while the samples from Colby, Mound Valley, Thayer, and Belleville were of much higher baking quality. The normally expected differences in protein quality among varieties were altered considerably by effects of environment during the growth of the samples studied.

The summer of 1956 was extremely hot and dry, and it is assumed that these conditions caused the observed differences in flour quality. Finney and Meyer (11) have shown that subnormal loaf volume, water absorption, and mixing properties were consistently associated with high temperatures

11

Table 1. Summary of analytical, physical dough testing, and baking data for the flour samples.

| Station | Jackson;Pawnee;Ponca;Comanche;Red Chief; Ave.: | | | | | | Kloon;Pawnee;Ponca;Comanche;Red Chief; Ave. | | | | | |

Flour Protein (14% M.B.)

Station						
Manhattan	17.3	17.4	17.3	16.5	17.1	17.1
Hays	17.2	15.5	16.3	15.6	15.3	16.0
Colby	14.3	14.1	14.3	13.7	13.8	14.2
Garden City	15.2	14.9	14.9	14.7	14.1	14.8
Mound Valley	11.3	12.1	10.7	11.0	10.6	11.1
Thayer	12.7	13.1	12.7	12.5	13.1	12.8
Belleville	13.1	12.9	12.9	12.2	13.1	12.0
Canton	15.7	17.0	15.5	16.1	15.2	15.9
Average	14.7	14.7	14.3	14.0	14.0	14.3

Flour Ash (14% M.B.)

Station						
Manhattan	0.41	0.42	0.43	0.43	0.44	0.42
Hays	0.48	0.43	0.49	0.49	0.45	0.46
Colby	0.44	0.43	0.47	0.44	0.44	0.44
Garden City	0.44	0.42	0.47	0.44	0.42	0.43
Mound Valley	0.39	0.39	0.41	0.39	0.42	0.40
Thayer	0.40	0.42	0.39	0.37	0.37	0.39
Belleville	0.39	0.39	0.36	0.38	0.38	0.38
Canton	0.41	0.46	0.48	0.44	0.48	0.46
Average	0.42	0.42	0.45	0.41	0.43	0.42

Mixogram Mixing Time (minutes)

Station						
Manhattan	3.50	2.75	2.75	4.50	3.50	3.40
Hays	3.50	3.00	3.00	2.75	2.75	2.95
Colby	4.50	4.00	2.75	3.00	3.00	3.15
Garden City	3.00	3.50	4.00	2.25	3.00	2.50
Mound Valley	4.25	1.75	3.75	2.75	2.75	3.05
Thayer	4.00	2.10	4.00	3.00	2.50	3.18
Belleville	5.00	2.87	3.50	3.00	3.00	3.47
Canton	5.25	2.75	6.00	4.00	2.75	3.95
Average	4.00	2.47	3.69	3.16	2.91	3.24

Farinograph Mixing Time (minutes)

Station						
Manhattan	9.00	9.25	9.25	11.50	8.00	9.40
Hays	8.75	5.25	6.75	6.00	4.75	6.70
Colby	11.00	6.00	7.50	6.25	5.50	7.25
Garden City	7.50	5.00	5.50	7.75	6.25	6.40
Mound Valley	8.00	4.50	5.00	5.25	5.00	5.55
Thayer	7.75	5.50	8.50	6.25	5.00	6.60
Belleville	11.00	5.75	8.00	7.50	6.00	7.65
Canton	10.50	10.00	12.00	13.50	7.50	10.70
Average	9.19	6.11	7.80	8.25	6.00	7.53

Loaf Volume (c.c.)

Station						
Manhattan	915	1050	1040	1020	970	1005
Hays	907	900	965	910	808	930
Colby	912	992	952	957	707	966
Garden City	830	867	835	837	837	861
Mound Valley	925	895	840	840	702	855
Thayer	915	917	882	875	847	899
Belleville	912	957	970	950	925	913
Canton	1022	932	985	950	922	962
Average	915	953	934	924	880	928

Gluten Quality Score

Station						
Manhattan	45	52	52	52	47	50
Hays	13	55	55	48	11	48
Colby	55	44	60	64	14	57
Garden City	8	13	45	43	13	48
Mound Valley	72	70	70	73	69	75
Thayer	58	68	63	63	55	64
Belleville	58	75	72	77	65	69
Canton	58	45	55	50	51	58
Average	59		60	60	52	

(above 90°F.) during the last 15 days of ripening. High temperatures did not always impair protein quality, however, because of mitigating physical conditions in the soil or relatively high humidity. Varieties with long mixing times were found to be more tolerant to the detrimental effects of high temperature during fruiting than were varieties with short mixing requirements.

It is commonly accepted that the protein content of wheat flours is the principle factor determining their bread-baking properties. Since the protein content of the samples vary from 10.6 to 17.4, a direct comparison of the baking performance of more than a few of the samples was not possible. For this reason, a simple numerical protein quality value was required. Finney (8) has shown that the relation between protein content and loaf volume is substantially linear for each variety between the limits of 8 and 20 percent protein for samples grown under normal conditions, and provided an adequate baking formula is used.

Since regression of loaf volume on protein content varies with variety, the loaf volume vs. protein content regression lines for varieties represent differences in protein quality. Using this system of variety regression lines, Finney and Farmers (10) developed a method of correcting experimentally obtained loaf volumes to a constant protein basis. Pence, et. al. (31) used the coefficient of regression of loaf volume on flour protein as a measure of the baking quality of flour proteins.

In the present work, the graph (10) developed by Finney for correcting loaf volumes to a constant protein basis was used to assign a baking quality score to each sample. The slope of the line on which the point representing the experimentally determined flour protein and loaf value coincided was assigned as the gluten quality score of the sample. Protein, loaf volume, and gluten quality score data in Table 1 indicate that this method ranked the samples in the proper order of flour quality based on a consideration of flour protein and loaf volume.

Composition of the Flour Fractions

Data for protein, total ash, and elemental composition of the flour fractions are presented in Tables 2 to 10. Results of analyses of variance of ash and elemental composition of the flour fractions as related to location and variety are presented in Table 11. Environment was the predominant factor, while variety played a secondary role in determining the elemental composition of the flour fractions. The differences in elemental composition related to environment and variety may be observed from the average values for the fractions recorded in Tables 2 through 10.

The flour protein was distributed among the complexes as follows: water-solubles 7 percent, gluten 83 percent, and starch 10 percent. Protein content of the water-solubles varied from 13.1 to 25.0 and averaged 18.5 percent. Protein in the starch ranged from 1.0 to 3.4 and averaged 1.7 percent. Protein in the gluten ranged from 54.1 to 69.1 and averaged 60.4 percent. This value for protein content of the gluten is lower than that reported by Sullivan (38) who listed the following average gluten composition: protein, 73 percent; lipides, 7.1 percent; starch, 5.1 percent; and ash, 0.60 percent. These values, however, were based on a procedure in which buffer solutions were used to wash glutens from doughs mixed to optimum development and are not directly comparable to this work.

The water-solubles contained 40, the gluten 20, and the starch 40 percent

Table 2. Summary of protein analyses for water-solubles, gluten, and starch fractions of the flours.

Station	Gms protein in the fraction from 100 gms of flour (14% M.b.)						Protein as percent of the flour fraction (14% M.b.)					

Water-Solubles

Station												
Manhattan	0.89	0.90	0.00	0.75	0.67	0.02	25.0	23.2	20.3	19.6	17.2	21.1
Hays	0.66	0.65	0.66	0.77	0.65	0.00	23.1	17.2	19.7	10.0	11.7	18.5
Colby	0.83	0.77	0.77	0.79	0.61	0.75	21.5	21.7	18.1	10.9	16.0	18.5
Garden City	0.92	0.56	0.55	0.57	0.76	0.09	19.9	20.9	16.6	20.1	13.7	19.9
Hosal Valley	0.61	0.60	0.62	0.83	0.91	0.03	10.5	10.6	16.5	17.2	13.7	16.9
Thayer	0.77	0.80	0.83	0.85	0.63	0.72	15.7	10.4	10.7	19.7	13.1	17.3
Belleville	0.76	0.72	0.78	0.70	0.70	0.76	16.9	18.1	17.6	16.9	13.1	16.15
Canton	0.66	0.65	0.61	0.61	0.60	0.61	21.6	20.3	18.1	19.0	11.9	10.9
Average	0.64	0.66	0.64	0.61	0.71	0.61	20.3	19.5	18.8	18.7	11.9	18.5

Gluten

Station												
Manhattan	14.13	11.95	12.01	11.69	11.74	12.30	65.9	59.6	55.6	50.8	55.6	59.9
Hays	9.72	9.57	12.18	10.19	10.35	10.55	65.5	63.0	59.3	60.7	59.1	61.7
Colby	9.45	9.27	9.23	7.23	9.45	8.95	60.1	63.0	57.6	60.3	58.1	61.3
Garden City	8.96	9.16	9.71	9.10	6.55	9.11	67.5	61.4	60.7	60.0	57.0	57.1
Hosal Valley	6.13	6.85	6.07	5.13	5.62	6.21	63.9	61.7	57.6	62.8	57.0	61.4
Thayer	7.54	8.04	7.54	7.15	8.15	7.57	57.7	57.7	50.7	62.3	55.4	59.3
Belleville	10.53	8.03	7.24	6.70	8.45	7.73	66.2	44.17	60.3	66.0	62.3	61.5
Canton	10.53	11.44	10.40	10.52	10.54	10.08	66.2	59.7	56.3	55.7	55.6	56.6
Average	9.32	9.40	9.35	8.65	9.40	9.23	65.7	59.7	58.3	60.5	57.5	60.1

Starch

Station												
Manhattan	0.72	0.74	0.63	0.72	0.63	0.70	1.2	1.3	1.2	1.2	1.1	1.2
Hays	0.92	1.20	1.17	1.11	0.74	1.02	1.7	2.0	2.0	1.8	1.1	1.7
Colby	1.07	1.19	1.16	2.31	0.67	1.28	1.7	1.5	1.8	3.4	1.3	2.0
Garden City	0.85	0.99	1.39	0.03	0.03	0.92	1.7	2.1	2.0	3.3	2.0	1.5
Hosal Valley	1.11	1.64	1.39	2.11	1.50	1.61	2.5	2.4	1.5	3.3	1.1	2.3
Thayer	1.78	1.17	0.96	1.09	0.63	1.14	2.6	2.4	2.7	1.6	1.1	1.7
Belleville	1.31	1.53	1.72	1.22	0.83	1.51	2.0	2.1	1.6	2.7	1.0	2.2
Canton	0.72	0.35	0.71	1.01	0.64	0.63	1.2	1.5	1.5	1.6	1.0	1.7
Average	1.05	1.16	1.14	1.14	0.84	1.12	1.7	1.8	1.9	2.1	1.2	1.7

Table 3. Distribution of ash in the water-solubles, gluten, and starch fractions of the flours.

Station	Milligrams of ash in the fractions from 100 grams of flour (14% M.B.)						Milligrams of ash per gram of fraction (14% M.B.)					
	Eleon	Pawnee	Ponca	Comanche	Red Chief	Avg.	Eleon	Pawnee	Ponca	Comanche	Red Chief	Avg.
Water-Solubles												
Manhattan	136	129	130	119	124	127	30.1	33.2	29.4	33.2	31.8	32.8
Hays	132	119	132	118	112	124	37.3	24.1	30.0	27.6	25.2	28.8
Colby	136	119	112	133	125	131	35.4	28.7	33.2	31.3	30.8	32.0
Garden City	129	122	115	126	135	131	28.0	27.4	31.5	29.8	30.0	29.3
Mound Valley	111	136	157	116	153	117	31.6	28.0	31.8	30.1	23.8	29.0
Thayer	111	131	127	126	115	128	28.6	26.1	30.7	29.3	23.8	27.7
Belleville	127	111	125	118	115	120	28.1	25.6	20.6	25.4	21.6	25.9
Canton	128	124	129	123	124	129	32.5	29.5	30.5	25.0	27.2	30.0
Average	135	122	138	127	125	130	32.5	27.0	30.7	29.4	26.7	29.1
Gluten												
Manhattan	74	80	82	72	96	82	3.4	3.9	3.0	4.0	4.5	3.9
Hays	57	82	101	74	95	77	3.9	3.7	5.0	4.3	5.1	4.4
Colby	61	67	76	83	83	66	3.7	4.4	4.7	4.4	5.1	4.5
Garden City	30	77	64	70	78	74	4.5	4.6	4.1	4.1	3.8	4.6
Mound Valley	41	44	42	33	44	39	3.3	3.9	3.6	3.8	3.9	3.8
Thayer	41	59	52	46	62	49	3.5	3.6	3.9	3.5	3.9	3.7
Belleville	60	100	67	36	52	15	3.4	4.1	4.7	3.6	5.7	3.7
Canton	53	66	71	59	107	89	4.0	4.6	4.3	4.2	4.6	4.6
Average					77	65	3.7	4.1		4.0		4.2
Starch												
Manhattan	130	122	125	119	117	121	2.2	2.2	2.2	2.0	1.9	2.1
Hays	133	123	139	131	117	134	2.0	2.0	2.4	2.1	2.2	2.2
Colby	133	134	137	116	127	136	2.1	2.2	2.2	2.2	1.9	2.1
Garden City	125	122	129	123	120	125	2.0	2.0	2.1	2.0	1.9	2.0
Mound Valley	129	130	111	94	130	119	2.0	1.9	1.6	1.3	1.7	1.1
Thayer	135	121	124	121	119	121	2.0	1.9	1.9	1.8	1.8	1.9
Belleville	131	131	123	121	125	126	2.0	1.8	1.8	1.7	1.8	1.8
Canton	127	129	135	132	137	132	2.3	2.0	2.2	2.0	2.1	2.2
Average	130	127	128	123	129	128	2.1	2.1	2.1	1.9	1.9	2.0

Table 4. Distribution of phosphorus in the water-solubles, gluten, and starch fractions.

Station	Milligrams of phosphorus in the fraction from 100 grams of flour (14% M.B.)						Phosphorus as percentage of the ash					
	Kanred	Pawnee	Comanche	Red Chief	Chiefkan	Ave.	Kanred	Pawnee	Comanche	Red Chief	Chiefkan	Ave.
Water-Solubles												
Manhattan	13.10	12.90	10.86	8.64	12.40	11.58	9.65	9.98	8.35	7.26	10.02	9.05
Hays	15.65	16.15	15.54	11.03	14.11	11.73	11.27	13.79	11.82	10.09	12.64	11.92
Colby	12.66	12.80	12.90	12.18	12.29	12.57	9.28	10.78	9.11	9.15	9.61	9.63
Garden City	14.26	14.22	15.58	10.03	16.04	11.20	11.06	11.66	10.76	8.60	11.90	10.80
Mound Valley	11.70	11.09	13.44	9.68	11.19	12.08	8.10	8.16	8.57	6.64	9.45	8.20
Thayer	13.60	12.80	11.00	8.93	13.47	12.12	9.63	10.31	8.61	7.10	11.72	9.48
Belleville	11.12	12.74	10.83	8.44	13.45	11.38	9.11	11.39	8.55	7.19	11.73	9.58
Canton	15.15	15.35	14.41	11.68	14.70	11.27	11.86	12.37	10.36	9.10	11.94	11.13
Average	13.44	13.55	13.17	10.29	13.68	12.07	10.00	11.06	9.52	8.11	11.15	9.97
Gluten												
Manhattan	33.28	28.24	27.32	26.04	34.67	30.41	45.12	35.19	33.89	35.92	36.33	37.27
Hays	26.16	27.43	31.04	30.08	37.10	32.37	45.56	47.10	40.43	40.49	39.22	42.57
Colby	24.90	25.66	23.66	19.90	29.12	25.65	49.06	38.02	37.92	37.16	35.18	39.53
Garden City	24.90	29.11	32.78	27.46	31.28	29.11	46.72	37.86	39.11	39.11	39.85	39.40
Mound Valley	13.98	18.34	16.25	11.53	17.76	15.58	46.61	41.81	38.40	35.10	40.16	40.16
Thayer	18.13	19.96	20.62	17.78	23.00	19.89	44.26	40.36	39.51	41.98	37.40	40.70
Belleville	15.79	19.54	16.50	13.83	20.56	17.44	44.30	38.26	39.72	37.78	39.28	39.08
Canton	30.41	36.58	33.98	30.04	39.95	34.19	44.76	36.56	38.94	36.16	37.23	38.73
Average	23.57	25.61	27.21	22.33	29.13	25.58	44.58	39.13	38.50	37.99	38.08	39.72
Starch												
Manhattan	30.00	28.38	24.90	27.52	30.85	28.49	23.72	23.24	19.73	23.05	25.44	23.04
Hays	34.07	33.63	35.32	34.57	41.23	35.92	26.31	27.37	25.48	26.12	26.11	26.74
Colby	35.06	27.02	37.52	37.92	36.80	34.87	26.37	20.09	27.38	25.88	25.85	25.71
Garden City	31.80	33.92	36.19	31.93	36.70	34.11	25.66	27.52	28.05	25.95	28.72	27.26
Mound Valley	28.17	32.36	33.60	34.12	32.23	32.15	22.13	21.82	30.25	36.48	21.65	27.57
Thayer	28.66	29.17	31.52	31.44	30.24	30.38	22.12	21.73	25.52	25.99	24.51	24.51
Belleville	25.52	30.82	30.32	28.37	30.21	29.08	19.50	23.19	24.70	25.19	24.27	23.09
Canton	34.90	34.57	34.32	35.59	33.00	31.64	27.13	26.04	25.38	26.99	24.63	25.25
Average	31.30	31.21	32.95	32.68	34.10	32.46	21.97	24.69	25.01	26.70	26.32	25.53

Table 5. Distribution of iron in the water-solubles, gluten, and starch fractions.

Station	Micrograms of iron in the fractions from 100 grams of flour (14% M.B.)					Iron as percentage of the ash				
	Hard:Pawnee:Pawnee:Comanche:Red Chief: Avo.					Hard:Pawnee:Pawnee:Comanche:Red Chief: Avo.				
Water-Solubles										
Manhattan	4	44	35	44	12	0.01	0.04	0.04	0.04	0.05
Hays	103	72	67	72	74	0.07	0.07	0.04	0.07	0.05
Colby	66	74	57	89	63	0.05	0.06	0.03	0.05	0.05
Garden City	75	71	49	86	69	0.04	0.06	0.05	0.05	0.05
Mound Valley	62	72	77	90	72	0.04	0.04	0.05	0.03	0.05
Thayer	96	49	49	33	47	0.07	0.04	0.07	0.04	0.04
Belleville	28	60	89	109	128	0.02	0.02	0.09	0.04	0.07
Centon	91	63	119	96	67	0.07	0.04	0.05	0.07	0.07
Average	66	63	67	69	62	0.05	0.03	0.05	0.06	0.05
Gluten										
Manhattan	920	902	916	906	926	1.28	1.11	1.16	1.16	1.18
Hays	929	617	662	501	637	1.63	1.09	0.43	0.74	0.93
Colby	601	580	603	470	575	1.22	0.86	0.63	0.90	0.71
Garden City	592	632	556	320	600	0.92	0.82	0.71	0.70	0.63
Mound Valley	115	500	450	371	445	1.18	1.11	1.00	0.88	1.16
Thayer	157	516	450	143	180	1.22	1.01	1.08	1.10	1.00
Belleville	632	776	642	190	639	1.16	1.54	1.55	0.59	1.14
Centon	565	676	604	505	599	0.85	0.63	0.70	0.62	0.69
Average	443	661	631	505	622	1.28	1.03	0.74	0.90	1.02
Starch										
Manhattan	110	329	336	114	131	0.34	0.42	0.42	0.38	0.35
Hays	165	326	390	275	375	0.35	0.23	0.27	0.23	0.28
Colby	207	349	233	130	336	0.40	0.27	0.21	0.30	0.29
Garden City	302	335	320	317	326	0.22	0.23	0.25	0.22	0.26
Mound Valley	208	327	197	207	311	0.45	0.16	0.11	0.33	0.23
Thayer	350	327	136	331	375	0.25	0.26	0.22	0.24	0.27
Belleville	274	239	206	371	116	0.22	0.30	0.35	0.30	0.30
Centon	101	311	322	311	355	0.22	0.18	0.13	0.23	0.22
Average		311	322			0.31	0.27	0.23	0.23	0.23

Table 6. Distribution of potassium in the water-solubles, gluten, and starch fractions.

18

Station	Milligrams of potassium in the fractions from 100 grams of flour (14% M.b.)					Potassium as percentage of the ash				

Water-Solubles

Manhattan	33.19	33.42	38.67	35.08	37.24	20.1	29.7	29.7	29.1	28.4	29.2
Hays	37.75	31.67	35.95	27.93	33.41	27.2	25.6	27.4	29.6	25.0	27.1
Colby	30.82	34.01	41.09	34.43	30.10	28.1	29.3	29.4	30.4	27.5	29.0
Garden City	34.22	31.15	44.07	35.23	35.10	28.5	25.5	25.5	28.7	26.2	26.7
Mound Valley	13.33	15.44	15.29	42.21	44.06	30.3	33.4	30.7	30.2	27.2	30.1
Thayer	35.06	32.12	37.42	35.14	39.96	25.5	25.5	27.4	28.2	25.1	26.7
Belleville	36.20	28.26	37.06	34.77	28.90	28.5	25.8	29.3	28.6	25.2	27.7
Canton	36.12	32.10	39.01	36.61	33.16	28.3	25.9	20.7	28.7	27.5	27.8
Average	37.56	34.33	39.69	37.00	36.11	27.8	27.8	20.6	29.2	26.7	23.0

Gluten

Manhattan	3.47	6.41	8.63	7.87	7.13	4.63	6.69	10.66	10.06	9.26	8.63
Hays	2.90	3.44	8.10	5.72	5.32	4.57	6.11	6.18	7.21	6.99	6.00
Colby	1.90	4.77	6.21	6.32	4.42	3.86	7.02	6.32	7.69	7.69	6.65
Garden City	2.30	5.61	5.34	5.77	4.03	3.07	7.25	7.10	7.15	7.31	6.55
Mound Valley	0.74	3.04	3.52	2.11	2.12	3.14	6.00	8.24	6.10	5.44	6.04
Thayer	2.10	3.04	4.16	2.77	4.72	6.16	7.04	8.06	7.04	8.41	7.26
Belleville	1.56	2.03	2.17	1.92	3.63	3.73	5.61	5.26	5.37	5.00	5.17
Canton	4.51	9.53	8.76	7.04	2.31	6.77	9.59	10.21	9.47	6.90	5.57
Average	2.15	5.02	5.03	4.26	7.59	4.50	7.37	8.21	7.59	7.26	6.99

Starch

Manhattan	18.36	18.06	17.09	15.52	17.33	13.51	14.39	13.31	14.32	11.34	11.05
Hays	17.02	15.50	20.11	19.16	18.18	12.92	12.61	11.02	11.13	11.09	13.55
Colby	17.25	17.00	20.62	20.39	19.24	13.66	11.21	15.42	11.46	15.05	14.02
Garden City	16.11	17.01	19.07	16.94	17.66	13.32	13.09	15.13	11.00	15.25	14.32
Mound Valley	19.22	21.03	11.15	17.17	17.21	11.47	15.09	10.00	16.70	11.16	11.36
Thayer	21.20	16.65	20.71	16.57	17.03	16.02	15.19	16.43	15.73	11.19	15.57
Belleville	18.40	17.16	19.78	19.65	18.36	13.27	12.05	15.80	15.86	15.34	14.44
Canton	18.75	17.23	21.77	19.06	19.17	15.00	13.22	16.33	11.93	12.94	14.51
Average	18.32	17.02	19.18	18.04	18.41	11.07	11.06	11.40	11.99	11.50	14.11

Table 7. Distribution of manganese in the water-solubles, gluten, and starch fractions.

Station	Milligrams of manganese in the fraction from 100 grams of flour (AK N.D.)					Manganese as percentage of the ash				
	Hays	Manas	Concho	Chief	Avg.	Hays	Manas	Concho	Chief	Avg.
Water-Solubles										
Manhattan	0.24	0.27	0.20	0.24	0.23	0.18	0.21	0.16	0.20	0.18
Hays	0.22	0.23	0.23	0.21	0.20	0.16	0.19	0.18	0.13	0.16
Colby	0.21	0.21	0.26	0.17	0.22	0.17	0.17	0.13	0.13	0.17
Garden City	0.27	0.26	0.31	0.27	0.30	0.20	0.22	0.23	0.27	0.22
Mound Valley	0.23	0.24	0.25	0.21	0.25	0.20	0.13	0.16	0.18	0.17
Thayer	0.09	0.10	0.24	0.11	0.18	0.07	0.15	0.18	0.20	0.13
Belleville	0.20	0.19	0.25	0.13	0.16	0.16	0.17	0.20	0.01	0.13
Canton	0.18	0.12	0.19	0.19	0.18	0.16	0.09	0.14	0.17	0.11
Average	0.22	0.21	0.24	0.23	0.21	0.16	0.17	0.18	0.13	0.17
Gluten										
Manhattan	0.06	0.06	0.09	0.09	0.09	0.08	0.07	0.10	0.11	0.10
Hays	0.25	0.06	0.33	0.22	0.23	0.12	0.12	0.34	0.32	0.20
Colby	0.15	0.12	0.11	0.13	0.15	0.22	0.13	0.20	0.25	0.23
Garden City	0.15	0.27	0.24	0.15	0.22	0.22	0.14	0.31	0.40	0.29
Mound Valley	0.05	0.04	0.07	0.07	0.05	0.20	0.10	0.16	0.07	0.11
Thayer	0.05	0.05	0.07	0.08	0.06	0.11	0.09	0.15	0.09	0.12
Belleville	0.06	0.05	0.05	0.03	0.05	0.12	0.12	0.11	0.11	0.10
Canton	0.07	0.11	0.09	0.17	0.10	0.09	0.12	0.09	0.15	0.11
Average	0.11	0.09	0.11	0.13	0.12	0.20	0.14	0.19	0.18	0.17
Starch										
Manhattan	0.12	0.17	0.17	0.12	0.11	0.11	0.13	0.12	0.10	0.11
Hays	0.12	0.10	0.13	0.13	0.16	0.14	0.11	0.16	0.10	0.12
Colby	0.19	0.19	0.17	0.13	0.17	0.14	0.11	0.12	0.09	0.12
Garden City	0.12	0.26	0.29	0.26	0.19	0.20	0.20	0.23	0.20	0.19
Mound Valley	0.25	0.17	0.19	0.22	0.23	0.16	0.11	0.13	0.16	0.13
Thayer	0.19	0.13	0.13	0.13	0.17	0.14	0.13	0.15	0.15	0.15
Belleville	0.18	0.18	0.25	0.21	0.21	0.12	0.11	0.11	0.11	0.13
Canton	0.17	0.16	0.23	0.13	0.16	0.13	0.11	0.10	0.11	0.11
Average	0.17	0.18	0.21	0.17	0.18	0.13	0.11	0.14	0.13	0.11

Table 8. Distribution of magnesium in the water-solubles, gluten, and starch fractions.

Station	Milligrams of magnesium in the fractions (from 100 grams of flour (14% M.B.))						Magnesium as percentage of the ash					
	Mean	Kansas	Texas	Carahorita	Hard	Ave.	Mean	Kansas	Texas	Carahorita	Hard	Ave.
Water-Solubles												
Manhattan	10.59	12.64	12.30	16.09	9.72	12.32	7.77	10.07	9.70	13.35	7.95	9.77
Hays	11.16	12.64	11.39	13.24	11.54	12.03	7.54	11.01	8.36	11.18	10.20	9.76
Colby	10.78	13.25	16.19	13.03	12.10	13.25	7.28	11.09	11.31	10.29	9.81	9.96
Garden City	9.20	18.29	13.34	0.00	12.60	10.69	7.09	14.03	9.25	0.00	9.23	0.09
Mound Valley	12.66	11.13	13.03	1.94	13.08	10.69	8.95	0.16	0.95	1.51	9.06	7.33
Thayer	10.35	12.80	13.83	12.04	6.27	11.16	8.83	10.35	10.09	9.70	5.10	8.98
Belleville	9.02	11.36	7.07	7.85	7.15	8.55	6.96	10.32	5.46	6.71	6.44	7.18
Canton	9.82	10.08	6.44	12.93	14.10	10.75	8.44	8.13	4.83	10.08	11.36	8.50
Average	10.52	12.82	11.85	9.73	10.97	11.18	7.85	10.57	8.56	7.85	8.68	8.70
Gluten												
Manhattan	0.53	0.96	0.99	1.39	1.16	1.08	0.80	1.22	1.24	1.76	1.52	1.31
Hays	0.68	0.20	2.00	1.33	1.40	1.13	1.20	3.71	2.00	1.51	1.48	2.06
Colby	0.65	1.22	1.69	0.69	2.23	1.31	1.74	1.79	2.26	1.32	2.71	1.96
Garden City	0.85	0.72	1.01	0.93	1.10	1.00	1.36	0.93	1.34	1.42	1.79	1.37
Mound Valley	0.33	0.77	0.98	0.73	0.85	0.73	1.07	1.72	2.29	2.21	1.96	1.05
Thayer	0.78	0.98	1.00	1.11	1.25	1.04	1.93	2.14	2.10	2.64	2.10	2.14
Belleville	0.77	0.95	0.72	0.60	1.22	0.05	1.83	1.69	1.73	1.44	2.32	1.88
Canton	1.60	3.27	2.55	2.04	2.52	2.40	2.41	3.29	2.96	2.46	2.30	2.70
Average	0.81	1.13	1.38	1.12	1.54	1.20	1.55	2.12	2.00	1.92	2.03	1.92
Starch												
Manhattan	1.69	2.21	1.83	2.27	3.03	2.22	1.33	1.86	1.49	1.81	2.51	1.60
Hays	2.09	2.94	2.61	3.21	3.45	3.06	2.21	2.10	2.09	2.52	2.35	2.31
Colby	3.26	3.62	3.84	2.98	2.71	3.29	2.41	2.64	2.77	2.04	2.19	2.11
Garden City	2.85	0.63	2.21	1.76	1.22	2.07	2.24	1.57	1.70	1.12	0.93	1.63
Mound Valley	1.11	0.42	0.42	1.97	2.10	1.26	0.89	0.50	0.43	2.15	1.50	1.09
Thayer	1.92	2.27	2.32	2.53	2.53	2.32	1.50	1.64	1.84	2.04	2.10	1.06
Belleville	2.37	2.57	2.85	3.56	3.58	2.99	1.84	2.01	2.36	2.01	2.88	2.30
Canton	3.11	2.94	2.85	2.46	2.50	2.78	2.44	2.20	2.09	1.81	1.09	2.11
Average	2.10	2.44	2.39	2.59	2.66	2.50	1.66	1.92	1.85	2.03	2.04	1.95

Table 9. Distribution of sodium in the water-solubles, gluten, and starch fractions.

Station	Milligrams of sodium in the fraction from 100 grams of flour (14 M.B.)						Sodium as percentage of the ash					
	Mean	Pawnee	Ponca	Comdo	RedChief	Ave.	Mean	Pawnee	Ponca	Comdo	RedChief	Ave.
Water-Solubles												
Manhattan	3.02	2.71	3.26	3.50	3.11	3.13	2.22	2.10	2.50	2.94	2.54	2.46
Hays	3.00	3.22	3.74	3.00	3.25	3.24	2.16	2.70	2.80	2.55	2.91	2.62
Colby	2.75	3.06	3.17	2.95	2.65	2.92	2.02	2.50	2.21	2.21	2.12	2.23
Garden City	3.02	2.68	3.56	2.93	3.32	3.11	2.31	2.68	2.45	2.36	2.46	2.46
Mound Valley	1.91	1.99	3.23	3.57	5.23	3.18	1.34	1.47	2.15	2.15	3.40	2.11
Thayer	3.33	3.11	4.27	3.05	3.11	3.38	2.36	2.66	3.12	2.13	2.70	2.65
Belleville	2.75	2.98	2.64	2.70	3.50	2.91	2.17	2.67	2.09	2.30	3.06	2.46
Canton	2.77	3.51	3.36	3.08	3.34	3.34	2.19	2.63	2.11	2.40	3.18	2.60
Average	2.82	2.91	3.10	3.10	3.51	3.15	2.10	2.46	2.16	2.16	2.00	2.15
Gluten												
Manhattan	0.66	0.92	0.60	0.64	0.66	0.70	0.93	1.16	0.73	0.82	0.70	0.87
Hays	0.53	0.34	0.59	0.46	0.46	0.46	0.96	0.63	0.59	0.55	0.49	0.64
Colby	0.41	0.47	0.50	0.27	0.36	0.40	0.65	0.70	0.67	0.51	0.44	0.63
Garden City	0.37	0.57	0.31	0.30	0.51	0.41	0.58	0.74	0.11	0.46	0.66	0.57
Mound Valley	0.33	0.45	0.23	0.24	0.15	0.28	1.09	1.00	0.55	0.76	0.35	0.75
Thayer	0.32	0.56	0.42	0.23	0.42	0.39	0.77	0.96	0.82	0.56	0.70	0.76
Belleville	0.33	0.36	0.25	0.21	0.37	0.30	0.78	0.72	0.62	0.57	0.69	0.63
Canton	0.46	1.25	0.11	0.51	0.53	0.63	0.69	1.26	0.48	0.63	0.48	0.71
Average	0.43	0.62	0.11	0.35	0.13	0.45	0.83	0.90	0.61	0.61	0.56	0.70
Starch												
Manhattan	1.45	0.85	1.20	1.67	1.08	1.11	1.09	0.67	0.91	1.56	1.58	1.16
Hays	1.00	0.84	0.53	0.62	0.63	0.74	0.78	0.68	0.12	0.44	0.46	0.56
Colby	1.25	1.50	1.22	1.02	1.20	1.24	0.97	1.23	0.94	0.71	0.89	0.95
Garden City	1.09	0.90	0.86	0.69	1.63	1.03	0.89	0.74	0.66	0.63	1.29	0.94
Mound Valley	0.98	1.30	1.04	1.53	1.80	1.33	0.74	0.99	0.73	1.51	1.51	1.10
Thayer	1.30	0.87	1.09	1.02	0.88	1.05	0.97	0.68	0.83	0.90	0.74	0.82
Belleville	1.38	0.92	1.26	1.26	1.26	1.22	1.00	0.69	1.00	1.28	1.05	1.00
Canton	0.79	0.96	1.70	1.11	3.01	1.52	0.64	0.72	1.29	0.85	2.06	1.11
Average	1.16	1.02	1.12	1.13	1.54	1.19	0.89	0.80	0.85	0.99	1.20	0.94

Table 10. Distribution of calcium in the water-solubles, gluten, and starch fractions.

Station	Milligrams of calcium in the fractions: From 100 grams of flour (14% h.b.)						Calcium as percentage of the ash					
	Hamil	Furman	Peren	Combined	Herf.	Ave.	Hamil	Furman	Peren	Combined	Herf.	Ave.
Water-Solubles												
Manhattan	2.21	3.54	6.90	1.63	2.10	3.30	1.63	2.74	5.33	1.39	2.00	2.63
Hays	2.00	0.60	4.33	4.36	1.51	4.17	1.44	7.21	3.30	3.68	1.35	3.10
Colby	2.32	7.21	9.54	4.27	2.27	5.13	1.70	6.09	6.73	3.20	1.81	3.91
Garden City	2.09	6.23	7.18	2.90	2.25	5.15	1.62	5.11	4.96	2.36	1.66	3.15
Mound Valley	3.34	2.90	8.79	7.47	3.11	5.12	2.31	5.60	5.60	5.13	2.05	3.45
Thayer	2.50	6.82	6.82	3.70	2.55	4.43	1.82	5.49	4.98	2.94	2.24	3.49
Belleville	2.30	9.10	3.98	9.15	2.45	5.41	1.82	8.10	3.15	7.77	2.15	4.61
Canton	2.29	9.91	5.52	8.26	2.23	5.64	1.79	7.99	3.98	6.45	1.79	4.40
Average	2.39	6.76	6.55	5.23	2.36	4.60	1.77	5.62	4.76	4.12	1.88	3.63
Gluten												
Manhattan	3.22	1.51	1.45	1.15	2.13	1.95	4.46	1.92	1.78	1.48	2.55	2.44
Hays	1.77	1.11	2.00	1.24	0.89	4.40	3.12	1.93	1.96	1.70	0.95	1.94
Colby	1.11	2.14	2.01	1.09	1.66	1.60	2.24	3.14	2.69	2.03	2.01	2.13
Garden City	1.46	1.24	1.30	1.26	1.52	1.36	2.32	1.62	1.75	1.03	1.93	1.09
Mound Valley	1.46	2.08	1.26	1.92	1.59	1.66	4.92	4.65	2.95	5.81	3.57	4.38
Thayer	1.34	1.93	1.93	1.35	1.55	1.55	3.29	3.15	3.74	3.20	2.63	3.20
Belleville	1.37	1.52	1.69	1.39	1.50	1.49	3.27	3.00	4.03	3.85	2.69	3.42
Canton	1.55	1.63	1.57	2.33	1.42	1.74	2.35	1.64	1.81	2.02	1.35	3.42
Average	1.66	1.63	1.65	1.47	1.57	1.60	3.25	2.66	2.60	2.85	2.24	2.72
Starch												
Manhattan	1.51	1.53	1.48	1.67	1.38	1.51	1.17	1.26	1.23	1.36	1.13	1.23
Hays	1.55	1.50	1.64	1.79	1.49	1.59	1.13	1.23	1.18	1.38	1.03	1.19
Colby	1.82	1.87	1.95	1.90	1.47	1.60	1.34	1.35	1.38	1.34	1.17	1.32
Garden City	1.82	1.57	1.64	1.64	1.50	1.63	1.42	1.23	1.25	1.30	1.11	1.20
Mound Valley	1.83	1.91	1.60	1.75	1.95	1.61	1.46	1.49	1.70	1.95	1.18	1.62
Thayer	1.78	1.70	1.67	1.98	1.49	1.72	1.35	1.37	1.37	1.66	1.26	1.40
Belleville	1.61	1.72	1.66	2.33	1.61	1.67	1.17	1.30	1.50	1.05	1.25	1.47
Canton	1.45	1.58	1.70	1.96	1.48	1.63	1.17	1.22	1.23	1.50	1.07	1.24
Average	1.70	1.67	1.69	1.83	1.55	1.70	1.31	1.31	1.36	1.54	1.19	1.34

Table 11. Summary of F values from analyses of variance for the ash and elemental composition of the flour fractions.

	Water-Solubles		Other		Flour	
	Location	Varieties	Location	Varieties	Location	Varieties

Amount of ash and elemental composition of the fractions from 100 g. of flour (116 M. D.)

	Water-Solubles		Other		Flour	
	Location	Varieties	Location	Varieties	Location	Varieties
Ash	9.15**	10.70***	28.54***	11.85***	2.64*	0.83
Phosphorus	8.36***	16.21***	32.77***	7.01***	6.70***	1.92
Iron	2.67*	1.22	21.30***	7.64***	1.60	1.21
Potassium	15.23***	12.33***	20.11***	16.05***	0.52	1.07
Manganese	4.95**	3.48*	10.13***	0.96	2.17**	1.10
Magnesium	0.74	0.66	9.17***	4.30**	8.02***	0.42
Sodium	0.51	2.16	5.73***	4.22**	2.01	2.18
Calcium	0.73	9.49***	0.85	0.23	3.85**	5.57***

Ash as percent of the flour fractions (116 M. D.) and individual elements as percent of the ash from the flour fractions

	Water-Solubles		Other		Flour	
	Location	Varieties	Location	Varieties	Location	Varieties
Ash	4.12**	7.57***	9.73***	10.50***	11.23***	5.32***
Phosphorus	16.91***	23.13***	2.12	10.49***	2.25	1.11
Iron	2.62*	1.97	11.61***	7.01***	2.09	1.61
Potassium	5.31***	4.75**	11.26***	25.69***	0.33	0.66
Manganese	3.31*	3.03*	0.51***	0.97	4.00**	1.12
Magnesium	0.76	1.21	4.21**	1.67	5.09***	0.15
Sodium	1.30	3.75*	1.02	7.79***	2.05	2.05
Calcium	0.85	9.63***	7.97***	2.25	11.69***	11.39***

4

of the total flour ash. Ash content of the complexes varied greatly. The water-solubles were highest in ash content ranging from 21.6 to 38.1 and averaging 29.4 mg. per gram. The gluten complex contained from 3.3 to 5.7 and averaged 4.2 mg. of ash per gram. Starch was extremely low in ash ranging from 1.3 to 2.4 and averaging 2.0 mg. per gram. Location and varietal differences with respect to ash content of the water-solubles, gluten, and starch were highly significant.

The water-solubles contained approximately 18, the gluten 36, and the starch 46 percent of the total flour phosphorus. Phosphorus averaged 9.97 percent of the water-solubles ash, 39.72 percent of the gluten ash, and 25.53 percent of the starch ash. Location was responsible for the greatest variation in phosphorus content of the flour fractions. Location and varietal differences in phosphorus content of the water-solubles and gluten fractions were highly significant, while only locational differences were significant for the starch fraction. Percentagewise, location and variety differences in phosphorus content of the water-solubles ash were highly significant. Location differences in gluten ash were insignificant, but variations among varieties were highly significant. Differences in phosphorus content of the starch ash were insignificant for both varieties and locations.

Approximately 6 percent of the total iron was in the water-solubles, 62 percent in the gluten, and 32 percent in the starch complex. The water-solubles ash averaged 0.06 iron, the gluten ash 1.02 percent and the starch ash 0.28 percent. Locational differences in iron content of the water-solubles and water-solubles ash were significant at the 5 percent level. Variety and location differences were highly significant for iron content of the gluten

and gluten ash. There were no significant differences in the iron content
of the starch or starch ash.

The flour potassium was distributed among the complexes as follows:
61 percent in the water-solubles, 8 percent in the gluten, and 31 percent
in the starch. The water-solubles ash averaged 28.0 percent potassium, the
gluten ash 7.0 percent and the starch ash 14.4 percent. Potassium content
of the water-solubles and gluten of their ashes varied significantly with
location and variety. There were no significant differences in potassium
content of starch and starch ash.

Approximately 60 percent of the flour calcium was in the water-solubles
complex, the remainder was almost equally divided between the starch and
gluten. The water-solubles ash averaged 3.63 percent calcium, the gluten
ash 2.72 percent, and the starch ash 1.34 percent. Calcium content of the
water-solubles and water-solubles ash varied significantly with variety,
while the calcium content of the gluten ash varied significantly with
location. Both location and variety differences in calcium content of the
starch and starch ash varied significantly.

Two-thirds of the flour sodium was in the water-solubles complex, one-
fourth in the starch, and the remainder in the gluten. The water-solubles
ash averaged 2.45 percent sodium, but sodium was responsible for less than
one percent of the weight of the gluten and starch ashes. There were no
significant differences in sodium content of the water-solubles, but
varietal differences in sodium content of the water-solubles ash were
significant. Sodium content of the gluten varied significantly with variety
and location. In the gluten and gluten ash, only varietal differences were
significant for this element.

Three-fourths of the flour magnesium was recovered in the water-solubles, 8 percent in the gluten, and 17 percent in the starch. The water-solubles ash contained 8.78 percent magnesium, while the gluten and starch ashes contained less than 2 percent. Magnesium content of the gluten varied significantly with variety and location, but only significantly with location in the gluten ash.

Approximately 41 percent of the manganese in the flour was recovered in the water-solubles, 24 percent in the gluten, and 35 percent in the starch fraction. Manganese was responsible for less than 0.2 percent of the ash in the flour complexes. Concentration of this element varied significantly among locations in all three fractions. In the water-solubles ash, manganese varied significantly with respect to location and variety. In the gluten and starch ashes, significant differences in manganese were due to locational effects only.

Relationship Between Mineral Composition and Baking Quality

Correlations as high as +0.98 between flour protein and loaf volume have been reported in the literature (Miller and Johnson, 25). A similar correlation coefficient for the present data was +0.54, which, although significant, is insufficient for prediction purposes. This low figure provides further evidence that the protein quality of at least some of the samples used in this study was inferior. The correlation between flour ash and gluten quality (r=-0.569***) was comparable with that for flour protein and loaf volume (r=+0.542***).

It is well known that proteins bind salts with significant effects on their physical properties. Swanson (40) discussed the effects of various

salts on flour doughs and dispersibility of flour proteins. Data obtained
in the present work substantiates the contention that minerals have important
effects on flour proteins and gluten quality as reflected by protein content
and loaf volume.

The correlations between gluten quality score and total ash, and between
gluten quality score and elemental composition of the flour fractions are
summarized in Table 12. These data indicate that as the ash content of the
gluten increases, the gluten quality score decreases. The correlation
between these factors was -0.618. Each of the elements determined, except
calcium, contributed in this effect. Phosphorus, the major component of ash
(12-32%), apparently was the main factor in this effect on gluten quality.
The high correlation between ash content of the gluten and gluten quality
score, and between phosphorus content of the gluten and gluten quality score
(-0.84) suggests that either ash or phosphorus content of the gluten is more
reliable than flour protein for predicting the breadmaking quality of flour.
This is an observation which has not been reported previously. Further work
relating phosphorus content to quality appears warranted. The phosphorus
content of water-solubles and starch also were significantly and negatively
correlated with gluten quality score. This may indicate that the major
portion of flour phosphorus was combined in some way with the gluten during
mixing and thereby affected its physical characteristics.

The potassium, manganese, and calcium concentrations of the starch, and
potassium concentration of the water-solubles were correlated significantly
and positively with gluten quality score. This suggests that the binding
of these elements by the water-solubles and starch prevented them from having
a detrimental influence on gluten properties. Further work should be done

Table 12. Coefficients of correlation between gluten quality score, ash, and concentration (mg. in flour fraction from 100 g. flour) of certain inorganic elements in the flour fraction.

Variables Correlated	Degree of Freedom	Flour Fractions		
		Gluten r	Starch r	Water-Solubles r
Quality score vs. ash	38	-0.818**	n. s.	n. s.
Quality score vs. phosphorus	38	-0.844***	-0.395*	-0.410**
Quality score vs. iron	30	-0.518**	n. s.	n. s.
Quality score vs. potassium	38	-0.636***	+0.389**	+0.303*
Quality score vs. manganese	38	-0.637***	+0.474**	n. s.
Quality score vs. magnesium	38	-0.439**	n. s.	n. s.
Quality score vs. sodium	38	-0.521***	n. s.	n. s.
Quality score vs. calcium	38	n. s.	+0.570***	n. s.

n. s. = non-significant

to determine what effect mixing doughs to optimum development would have on the distribution of the various elements among the three flour complexes. It is possible that mechanical mixing, rather than the gentle treatment used in separation of the fractions for the present study, would cause more of the elements to combine with the gluten proteins. Conceivably, this might result in higher correlations between elemental composition of the gluten and gluten quality score.

SUMMARY AND CONCLUSIONS

This investigation of the mineral composition of gluten, starch, and water-solubles fractions of hard wheat flour and its relationship to flour quality has led to the following conclusions:

1. Environment was more important than variety in determining flour quality and mineral composition of the flour and flour fractions.

2. Gluten quality score gave a better measure of flour quality than did loaf volume.

3. Concentration of ash or phosphorus in the gluten was a better measure of flour quality than flour protein or loaf volume.

4. Mineral content of the flour and gluten was significantly and negatively correlated with gluten quality score. Each element determined, except calcium, contributed to this effect.

5. Phosphorus, iron, potassium, sodium, manganese, and magnesium concentration of the gluten were each significantly and negatively correlated with flour quality.

6. The concentration of phosphorus in the water-solubles was significantly and negatively correlated, while the potassium content was significantly and positively correlated with gluten quality score.

7. Concentrations of potassium, calcium, and magnesium in the starch were significantly and negatively correlated with gluten quality score.

8. In general, the elemental composition of gluten was more highly correlated with gluten quality score than was the elemental composition of water-solubles and starch.

SUGGESTIONS FOR FUTURE WORK

The investigation reported here was of the survey type. It was designed to determine specific areas for further and more intensive investigations. The results have suggested the following for future work:

1. A study of the relationships between phosphorus content of whole wheat and flour, and baking quality. These samples should include those high in protein, low in ash and low in quality. These can usually be obtained from Chillicothe and Denton, Texas, and certain stations in Oklahoma.

2. A study of the relationship between protein and phosphorus concentrations of bread type flours.

3. A study of the distribution of mineral elements in the gluten, water-solubles and starch separated from doughs mixed to optimum development.

4. A study of the concentrations and types of phosphorus occurring in flour and flour fractions.

5. A study of the relationships among sedimentation values, valorimeter values, phosphorus concentrations, and gluten quality score.

ACKNOWLEDGMENTS

The author wishes to acknowledge his indebtedness to Dr. Byron S. Miller, major instructor, and Dr. John A. Johnson for their constant aid and advice in carrying out this work and preparing the manuscript, and to Dr. John A. Shellenberger, Head, Department of Flour and Feed Milling Industries, for providing research facilities.

Special acknowledgments are due Karl F. Finney and Merle Shogren for providing laboratory facilities and guidance in preparing the flour fractions; to Dr. William O. Schrenk for providing laboratory facilities and assistance in carrying out the spectrochemical analyses; to Mr. Donald Miller for the experimental baking data; to Mr. O. D. Miller for advice and help with analytical problems.

Gratitude also is extended to the many individuals at Kansas State College, who so willingly offered counsel and advice throughout this work.

LITERATURE CITED

1. American Association of Cereal Chemists.
   Cereal laboratory methods, 6th ed. The Association: St. Paul,
   Minnesota, 1956.

2. Association of Official Agricultural Chemists.
   Official methods of analysis, 8th ed. The Association:
   Washington, D. C. 1955.

3. Bailey, C. H.
   Constituents of wheat and wheat products. Reinhold Publishing
   Company. New York, New York. 1944.

4. Beckman Instruments Incorporated.
   Instruction manual for D. U. and E. flame spectrophotometers.
   334-A. Fullerton, California. 1954.

5. Beeson, K. C.
   The mineral composition of crops with particular reference to the
   soils in which they were grown. U.S.D.A. Misc. Pub. 369. 1941.

6. Davidson, J., and J. H. Shollenberger.
   Effect of sodium nitrate applied at different stages of growth of
   wheat on the baking quality of flour. Cereal Chem. 3:137-143.
   1926.

7. El Gindy, M. M., C. A. Lamb, and R. C. Burrell.
   Influence of variety, fertilizer treatment, and soil on the protein
   content and mineral composition of wheat, flour, and flour fractions.
   Cereal Chem. 34:185-195. 1957.

8. Finney, K. F.
   Fractionating and reconstituting techniques as tools in wheat flour
   research. Cereal Chem. 20:381-396. 1943.

9. Finney, K. F.
   Contributions of the hard winter wheat quality laboratory to wheat
   quality research. Trans. Am. Assoc. Cereal Chem. 12:127-142. 1954.

10. Finney, K. F., and M. A. Barmore.
    Loaf volume and protein content of hard winter and spring wheats.
    Cereal Chem. 25:291-312. 1948.

11. Finney, K. F., and J. W. Meyer.
    Effect of high temperature and drought on wheat and flour properties.
    USDA. Misc. Pub. 241 CO. 1952.

12. Finney, K. F., M. D. Shogren, R. C. Hoseny, L. C. Bolte, M. H. Maurer, and J. A. Shellenberger.
Quality characteristics of hard winter wheat varieties grown in the Southern, Central, and Northern Great Plains of the United States 1956 crop. Hard Winter Wheat Quality Laboratory, Kans. Agri. Exp. Sta. Mimeo. report 437 CC. 1957.

13. Fisher, M. H., T. R. Aitkens, and J. A. Anderson.
Effects of mixing, salt, and consistency on extensograms. Cereal Chem. 26:81-97. 1949.

14. Gericke, W. F.
Effect of nitrate salts supplied to wheat grown in liquid media on bread scores. II. Cereal Chem. 11:141-152. 1934.

15. Gericke, W. F.
Effect of chloride salts supplied to wheat grown in liquid media on bread scores. III. Cereal Chem. 11:335-343. 1934.

16. Greaves, J. E., A. F. Bracken, and C. T. Hirst.
The influence of variety, season, and green manure upon the composition of wheats. Journ. Nutr. 19:178-186. 1940.

17. Greaves, J. E., and E. L. Carter.
The influence of irrigation water on the composition of grains and the relationship to nutrition. Journ. Biol. Chem. 58:531-541. 1923.

18. Harris, R. H., and L. D. Sibbit.
The comparative baking qualities of starches prepared from different wheat varieties. Cereal Chem. 18:585-604. 1941.

19. Harris, R. H., and L. D. Sibbit.
The comparative baking qualities of hard red spring wheat starches and glutens as prepared by the gluten-starch blend baking method. Cereal Chem. 19:763-772. 1942.

20. Johnson, J. A., R. O. Pence, and J. A. Shellenberger.
Milling and baking characteristics of hard winter wheat varieties of Kansas. Kans. Agr. Exp. Sta. Circ. 238. 1947

21. Johnson, J. A., C. O. Swanson, and E. G. Bayfield.
The correlation of mixograms with baking results. Cereal Chem. 20:625-644. 1943.

22. Mattern, P. J., and R. M. Sandstedt.
Influence of the water-soluble constituents of wheat flour on its mixing and baking characteristics. Cereal Chem. 34:252-267. 1957.

23. McCalla, A. C., and E. K. Woodford.
The effect of potassium supply on the composition and quality of wheat. II. Can. Journ. Res. 13 C:339-351. 1935.

24. Miller, D. S., Betts Hays, and John A. Johnson.
    Correlation of farinograph, mixograph, sedimentation, and baking data
    for hard red winter wheat flour samples varying widely in quality.
    Cereal Chem. 33:277-290. 1956.

25. Miller, D. S., and J. A. Johnson.
    A review of methods for determining the quality of wheat and flour
    for breadmaking. Kans. Agr. Exp. Sta. Tech. Bul. 76. 1954.

26. Miller, B. S., Joann Y. Sciffe, J. A. Shellenberger, and G. D. Miller.
    Amino acid content of various wheat varieties I. Cystine, lysine,
    methionine, and glutamic acid. Cereal Chem. 27:96-106. 1950.

27. Morris, V. H., T. L. Alexander, and E. D. Pascoe.
    Studies of the composition of the wheat kernel. III. Distribution of
    ash and protein in central and peripheral zones of whole kernels.
    Cereal Chem. 23:540-547. 1946.

28. Pence, J. W., A. H. Elder, and D. K. Mecham.
    Preparation of wheat flour pentosans for use in reconstituted doughs.
    Cereal Chem. 27:60-66. 1950.

29. Pence, J. W., A. H. Elder, and D. K. Mecham.
    Some effects of soluble flour components on baking behavior.
    Cereal Chem. 28:94-104. 1951.

30. Pence, J. W., D. K. Mecham, and H. S. Olcott.
    Review of proteins of wheat flour. Journ. Agr. & Food Chem. 4:712-716.
    1956.

31. Pence, J. W., N. E. Weinstein, and D. K. Mecham.
    The albumin and globulin contents of wheat flour and their
    relationship to protein quality. Cereal Chem. 31:303-311. 1954.

32. Pons, W. A., M. F. Stansbury, and C. L. Hoffpauir.
    An analytical system for determining phosphorus compounds in plant
    materials. Journ. Assoc. Off. Agr. Chem. 36:492-504. 1953.

33. Pyler, E. J.,
    Baking Science and technology, Volume II. Siebel Publishing Company.
    1952.

34. Standstedt, R. M., C. E. Jolitz, and M. J. Blish.
    Starch in relation to some baking properties of flour. Cereal
    Chem. 16:780-792. 1939.

35. Schronk, W. G.
    Chemical composition of Kansas wheat. Kans. Agr. Exp. Sta. Tech.
    Bul. 79. July, 1955.

36. Schrenk, W. G., and H. H. King.
Composition of three varieties of Kansas-grown wheat. Mineral analysis of wheat and soil. Cereal Chem. 25:61-71. 1948.

37. Sollars, W. F.
A new method of fractionating wheat flour. Cereal Chem. 33:111-120. 1956.

38. Sullivan, Betto.
Proteins in flour. Review of the physical characteristics of gluten and reactive groups involved in change of oxidation. Journ. Agr. & Food Chem. 2:1231-1234. 1954.

39. Sullivan, Betto, and Cleo Near.
Relation of the magnesium in the ash and the lipoid-protein ratio to the quality of wheats. Journ. Am. Chem. Soc. 49:467-472. 1927.

40. Swanson, C. O.
Physical properties of doughs. Burgess Publishing Company. 1946.

41. Swanson, C. O., and J. A. Johnson.
Description of mixograms. Cereal Chem. 20:39-42. 1943.

42. Wöstmann, B.
The cystine content of wheat flour in relation to dough properties. Cereal Chem. 27:391-397. 1950.

43. Yamazaki, W. T.
The concentration of a factor in soft wheat flours affecting cookie quality. Cereal Chem. 32:26-37. 1955.

APPENDIX

Preparation of Flour Fractions

Flour (250 g., 14% moisture basis) was shaken vigorously for one minute in a 2000 ml. Erlenmeyer flask with 550 ml. of cold (2-4°C) distilled water. The flour slurry was transferred to centrifuge tubes (one pint milk bottles) with 50 ml. of cold distilled water and centrifuged for 20 minutes at 1000 rpm in an International Centrifuge (Model V). The supernatant was decanted from one of the centrifuge bottles into a 2000 ml. enamel beaker. The dough was removed from this centrifuge bottle with a stainless steel spatula and placed in the decanted liquid. The supernatant from each succeeding centrifuge bottle was used to rinse the previously emptied bottle and the dough added to that in the enamel beaker.

The combined dough pieces from the 250 g. of flour were kneaded gently in the liquid until a good separation of gluten and starch was obtained. The gluten then was placed in a small bowl and the liquid containing the suspended starch passed through a 40 mesh silk cloth sieve. Any gluten remaining on the sieve was collected and added to the washed portion. The gluten was rewashed for two minutes in each of six successive 40 ml. aliquots of cold (2-4°C) distilled water. Each aliquot of wash water was passed through the sieve into the starch solution.

The washed gluten mass was placed in a refrigerator for one hour after which any remaining liquid was discarded, and the gluten weighed and sliced into long strips. These strips were frozen on the interior of wide-mouthed, quart Mason jars which previously had been cooled to approximately -70°C. on dry ice. The gluten strips were spread quickly to cover a large area using stainless steel crucible tongs. The frozen gluten was stored in a deepfreeze at -20°C. until lyophilized.

The water-solubles were separated from the starch by passing the starch suspension through a Sharples Super-Centrifuge (Type T 1), the speed of which was controlled by a "Variac". Approximately one-half of the starch suspension was passed through the centrifuge at one-half speed in order to spread the starch evenly within the rotating cylinder. The speed was then increased to full for 3 minutes to pack the starch, after which it was reduced to one-half. The remaining starch suspension was passed through at this setting. The centrifuge was rinsed with 25 ml. of distilled water and the liquid (water-soluble) fraction measured. Duplicate 10 ml. aliquots were taken for protein analysis and the remainder was shell-frozen immediately on the interior of a one gallon glass jar by mechanically rotating the jar in methyl-cellosolve (ethylene glycol monomethyl ether) cooled to -70°C. with dry ice. The frozen solution was stored at -20°C. until lyophilized.

The starch and dextrin fractions were removed from the centrifuge, weighed, placed on a glass plate, and mixed thoroughly with a large stainless steel spatula. Drying at room temperature was accelerated by frequent sub-dividing and mixing under a current of air from a fan.

The frozen gluten and water-solubles were dried by lyophilizing at a pressure between 50 and 100 microns.

Ashing Methods (1)

New Coors No. 170 porcelain crucibles were used for ashing the samples. Prior to use, they were heated in a muffle furnace at 520°C. for 16 hours. After cooling, they were washed in concentrated hydrochloric acid and rinsed in distilled water.

An appropriate amount of sample was weighed into a crucible and placed

in a muffle furnace adjusted to 520°C. To prevent the starch and gluten
samples from puffing out of the crucibles, it was necessary to ignite the
first vapors given off. The samples were allowed to remain in the furnace
until carbon-free. The starch and water-solubles samples required 12 to 18
hours. Many gluten samples required heating for 72 hours. The ash was
weighed and stored in glass vials until analysis for minerals could be made.

Determination of Total Phosphorus (32)

Preparation of Solutions. The concentrated reduced molybdate reagent
was prepared by weighing 39.12 g. of reagent grade molybdic anhydride into
a round bottomed pyrex flask, adding 800 ml. of concentrated sulfuric acid,
and heating at 150°C. with stirring, until solution was complete, as
indicated by a clear, greenish color. After the quantitative addition of
2.2 g. of powdered molybdenum metal (99.5 percent Mo), heating and stirring
was resumed until solution was complete. The deep-blue solution was cooled,
transferred quantitatively to a one liter volumetric flask, and diluted to
volume with concentrated sulfuric acid.

The dilute reduced molybdate solution was prepared by pipetting 10 ml.
of the concentrated reduced molybdate reagent into a 100 ml. volumetric
flask containing about 50 ml. of distilled water. The pipette was rinsed
with distilled water, the rinsings added to the flask, and the solution
diluted to volume with distilled water. A fresh solution of this reagent
was prepared each day.

The concentrated stock phosphate solution was prepared by dissolving
4.3929 g. of A. C. S. grade dry monobasic potassium phosphate in 300 ml. of
distilled water and 200 ml. of 1 N sulfuric acid contained in a one liter

volumetric flask. Several drops of 0.1 N potassium permanganate were added and the solution diluted to volume with distilled water. This solution contained 1.0 mg. of phosphorus per ml. and was found to be stable.

The diluted stock phosphate solution containing 0.01 mg. of phosphorus per ml. was prepared by diluting the concentrated stock solution 1:100. A fresh solution of this reagent was prepared each day.

Digestion of Samples. An appropriate amount of sample (300 mg. of water-solubles, 300 mg. of gluten, or 400 mg. of starch) was weighed into a 100 ml. Micro-Kjeldahl flask. Three ml. of concentrated sulfuric acid and two, 6 mm., glass beads were added. The sample was heated until all organic material was charred and a homogenous solution obtained. After cooling, four drops of 30 percent hydrogen peroxide were added and the solution was heated until colorless. It usually was necessary to add additional peroxide up to a total of 10 drops with intermittent heating and cooling. The solution was heated for 10 minutes after the last addition of peroxide. When cool, 20 ml. of water was added and the solution boiled for 5 minutes to remove remaining peroxide and insure conversion of phosphorus to the ortho form. After cooling, the solution was quantitatively transferred to a 100 ml. volumetric flask and diluted to volume. This sample solution was used for the colorimetric determination of phosphorus.

Colorimetric Determination of Phosphorus. A suitable aliquote of the sample solution (standard phosphate, 5 ml. of water-solubles, 10 ml. of starch, or 10 ml. of gluten solution) was transferred to a 100 ml. volumetric flask. Sufficient 3.60 N sodium hydroxide was added to neutralize the acidity. Two drops of indicator, 0.2 percent aqueous solution of sodium alizarin sulfonate, were added and the acidity adjusted with 1.0 N sulfuric acid and 1.0 N sodium hydroxide until one drop of the acid turned the solution yellow. The solution was then diluted to approximately 70 ml. with distilled water. A reagent blank was prepared using the same amount of 3.60 N alkali as for the samples and the acidity adjusted in the same manner. A ten ml. aliquot of the reduced molybdate reagent was added to the blank and each sample solution. All flasks were mixed by swirling and placed in a boiling water bath for exactly 30 minutes. After cooling in a cold water bath, the reaction solutions were diluted to volume with distilled water. Intensity of the color was read in a Bausch and Lomb "Spectronic 20" colorimeter at 820 mµ. Using the reagent blank, the instrument was set at 100 percent transmission. Milligrams of phosphorus in the sample aliquot was determined by reference to the standard curve.

Preparation of Calibration Curve. Aliquots of 0.0, 1.0, 2.0, 3.0, 4.0, 5.0, 6.0, 7.0, 8.0, 10.0, and 12.0 ml. of the diluted phosphate solution (0.01 mg. of phosphorus per ml.) were pipetted into 100 ml. volumetric flasks. Two drops of indicator and one drop of 1 N sulfuric acid were added and the solution diluted to approximately 70 ml. with distilled water. After adding 10 ml. of reduced molybdate solution, the procedure outlined above for treatment of the sample aliquot was followed. The standard containing no phosphorus was used to set the instrument at 100 percent transmission. The logarithms of the transmittance values obtained for the standards were plotted against the known phosphorus concentrations to obtain the calibration curve.

Quantitative Estimation of Iron (2)

Preparation of Solutions. The complexing reagent was prepared by dissolving 0.1 g. of alpha, alpha-dipyridyl in distilled water and diluting to 100 ml. with water.

The reducing solution was prepared by diluting 10 g. of hydroxylamine hydrochloride to 100 ml. with water.

The acetate buffer was prepared by diluting 8.3 g. of anhydrous sodium acetate (previously dried at 100°C) and 12 ml. of glacial acetic acid to 100 ml. with water.

Preparation of Reference Curve. The concentrated stock solution of iron was prepared containing 3.512 grams of iron ammonium sulfate-hexahydrate and two drops of concentrated hydrochloric acid per 500 ml. of solution. The final stock solution containing 0.01 mg. of iron per ml. was prepared by diluting 10.0 ml. of the concentrated stock solution to one liter.

The standard iron solutions consisted of 2.0, 5.0, 10.0, 15.0, 20.0, 25.0, 30.0, 35.0, 40.0, and 45.0 ml., respectively, of the final diluted iron stock solution and 2.0 ml. of concentrated hydrochloric acid diluted to 100 ml. with water. The blank solution contained 2.0 ml. of concentrated hydrochloric acid diluted to 100 ml. with distilled water. Ten ml. of each of the standard iron solutions and the blank were used in the procedure involving one colorimetric determination of iron (Appendix).

Preparation of Sample Solutions. An appropriate amount of flour fraction (5 g. of gluten, 5 g. of starch, or 2 g. of water-solubles) was ashed according to the method given in the appendix. The ash residues were dissolved in 2 ml. of concentrated hydrochloric acid and evaporated to dryness. Each residue was taken up in 2 ml. of concentrated hydrochloric acid, warmed gently, filtered quantitatively into a volumetric flask (25 ml. for gluten and starch, 50 ml. for water-solubles), and diluted to volume with water. Whatman No. 42 filter paper was used.

Colorimetric Determination of Iron. An appropriate aliquot of the sample solution (10 ml. water-solubles, 3 ml. gluten, or 15 ml. starch) was pipetted into a 25 ml. volumetric flask, and 1.0 ml. of hydroxylamine hydrochloride added. After standing for a few minutes, 5.0 ml. of the acetate buffer solution and 2.0 ml. of the alpha, alpha-dipyridyl solution were added and the solution diluted to volume. The solutions were allowed to stand for 30 minutes, and the intensity of color in each was read in a Bausch and Lomb "Spectronic 20" colorimeter at 515 mµ. The blank solution was used to set the instrument at 100 percent transmission. The iron concentration of these solutions were determined from the calibration curve.

Flame Photometry (4)

Instrument. A Beckman Model D. U. spectrophotometer equipped with a Beckman 9200 flame photometry attachment and Beckman atomiser-burner assembly was used.

Sample Preparation. Known quantities of ash were dissolved in 2.0 ml. of concentrated hydrochloric acid and evaporated just to dryness on a hot-plate. The residue was taken up in exactly 2.0 ml. of concentrated hydro-chloric acid, and warmed gently on a hot-plate. The solutions of ash from the water-solubles were filtered and made up to 50.0 ml. with distilled water. The solutions from the starch and gluten were made up to 25 ml. with distilled water. These solutions were stored in a refrigerator to prevent mold growth.

Stock Solutions. The stock solutions for preparation of the standard solutions were prepared according to the following:

Stock Solutions	Concentration of the element μg/ml.	Salt Used	Weight of Salt g./liter
Sodium	1000	NaCl	2.542
Potassium	1000	KCl	1.907
Calcium	1000	CaCO₃*	2.497
Manganese	200	MnCl₂·4H₂O	0.720
Magnesium	5000	Mg(C₂H₃O₂)₂·4H₂O*	44.093

* The salt was dissolved in 6.0 N hydrochloric acid, heated gently, and quantitatively transferred to a one liter volumetric flask.

Preparation of Standard Solutions. The material remaining after the moisture determinations was composited according to fraction, mixed, ashed, and analyzed. This information was useful in determining the concentrations of interferring ions necessary for the standard solutions.

The standard solutions were prepared by appropriate dilutions of the stock solutions. Each contained the interferring elements in the approximate concentration expected in the sample solutions, and hydrochloric acid in the same concentration as in the sample solutions. At least 4 ml. of concentrated hydrochloric acid per 100 ml. of standard was necessary to inhibit mold growth. Up to 8 ml. of the acid per 100 ml. gave satisfactory results.

The standard solutions for preparation of the standard curve were prepared according to the following:

Element Analyzed	Range of Standards μg/ml.	Interferring elements added	Remarks
Potassium	0-100	Sodium	
Sodium	0-100	Potassium	Range reduced when concentration of samples permitted.
Calcium	0-100	Sodium, and Potassium	Range reduced when concentration of samples permitted.

Element Analyzed	Range of Standards µg/ml.	Interferring elements added	Remarks
Manganese	0-20	Sodium, Potassium, and Calcium	Range could be extended when necessary.
Magnesium	0-250	Sodium, Potassium, and Calcium	

Operation of the Flame Photometer. An oxygen-acetylene flame was used with an acetylene pressure of four pounds per square inch and the oxygen pressure recommended for the burner. The red-sensitive phototube was used with a 2000 megohm resistor. The instrument was operated with the selector switch at the 0.1 position and the photomultiplier set on "full". The slit-width was adjusted to give a reading of 100 percent transmission when the most concentrated standard was atomized with the sensitivity control set near the counter-clockwise limit. The sensitivity control seldom needed further adjustment if the dark-current remained properly adjusted.

Readings were made on each standard, beginning with the least concentrated one. A standard curve was prepared by plotting the average of duplicate readings for each standard against the element concentration in µg. per ml.

Successive readings were made on four to ten sample solutions depending on stability of the instrument. The instrument adjustment was checked after each sample group by reading several standards covering the concentration range of the sample solutions. The series of samples was re-read in reverse order. Whenever duplicate readings varied by more than one percent trans-mission, the instrument adjustment was checked and the samples read again. Concentrations of the sample solutions were determined by reference to the standard curve.

Wavelengths and approximate slit-widths used for measuring the elements were as follows:

Element	Wavelengths	Slit-width
	mμ.	mm.
Potassium	770	0.11
Sodium	589	0.0125
Calcium	554	0.040
Manganese	403.3	0.045
Magnesium	383.0	0.050

MINERAL COMPOSITION OF GLUTEN, STARCH, AND WATER-SOLUBLES
FRACTIONS OF WHEAT FLOUR AND ITS RELATIONSHIP TO FLOUR QUALITY

by

ROBERT KEEBLER BEQUETTE

B. S., Montana State College, 1956

AN ABSTRACT OF A THESIS

submitted in partial fulfillment of the

requirements of the degree

MASTER OF SCIENCE

Department of Flour and Feed Milling Industries

KANSAS STATE COLLEGE
OF AGRICULTURE AND APPLIED SCIENCE

1958

The influence of environment and variety on the total ash and elemental composition of the water-solubles, gluten, and ash complexes separated from forty hard red winter wheat flour-water suspensions, and the relationship of these factors to flour quality was investigated. Iron content of the fractions was determined colorimetrically using alpha, alpha-dipyridyl as the complexing agent. Total phosphorus was determined by a reduced molybdate colorimetric procedure. Sodium, calcium, potassium, manganese, and magnesium were determined with a Beckman D. U. Spectrophometer equipped with a flame photometry attachment.

Results of analytical, physical dough, and baking tests on the flour samples indicated that many of the samples contained abnormal protein due to environmental conditions during ripening. The coefficient of regression of loaf volume on flour protein was used as a measure of baking quality and designated gluten quality score. This score proved to be a better index of flour quality than loaf volume. Location was more important than variety in determining flour quality and mineral composition of the flour and flour fractions.

The correlation between flour ash and gluten quality score (r=-0.569***) was comparable with that for flour protein and loaf volume (r=+0.542***). Correlations between gluten quality score and total ash, and between gluten quality score and elemental composition of the flour fractions indicate that as the ash content of the gluten increases, the gluten quality score decreases. Each of the elements determined, except calcium, contributed in this effect.

The potassium, manganese, and calcium concentrations of the starch and potassium concentration of the water-solubles were correlated significantly and positively with gluten quality score. This suggests that the binding of these elements by the water-solubles and starch prevents them from having a detrimental influence on gluten properties.

Phosphorus, the major component of ash (12-32%), apparently was the main element affecting gluten quality. The high correlation between the ash content of the gluten and gluten quality score (-0.818) and between phosphorus content of the gluten and gluten quality score (-0.84) suggests that either ash or phosphorus content of the gluten was more reliable than flour protein or loaf volume for predicting the breadmaking quality of flour. The phosphorus contents of water-solubles and starch also were significantly and negatively correlated with gluten quality score. This may indicate that the major portion of flour phosphorus was combined in some way with the gluten during mixing and thereby affected its physical characteristics.

CPSIA information can be obtained
at www.ICGtesting.com
Printed in the USA
BVHW040527161121
621753BV00008B/236